A PROBLEM OF EVIL

A PLAY IN TWO ACTS
By RC ATCHISSON

Copyright 2011

Copyright © 2011 by RC Atchisson

All rights reserved. This work or any portion thereof may not be reproduced or used in any manner whatsoever without the express written permission of the publisher except for the use of brief quotations in a book review.

Printed in the United States of America
ISBN-10: 0-9974144-1-3
ISBN-13: 978-0-9974144-1-7

Library of Congress Control Number: 2016904907

For rights and royalty information contact:
Stingy Brim LLC
St. Louis, MO 63123
stingybrimllc@rcatchisson.com
www.rcatchisson.com

Cover Design by Jessica Sturgeon

This is a work of fiction. Names, characters, businesses, places, events and incidents are either the products of the author's imagination or used in a fictitious manner. Any resemblance to actual persons, living or dead, or actual events is purely coincidental.

Finally, be strong in the Lord and in the strength of his might. Put on the whole armor of God, that you may be able to stand against the schemes of the devil. For we do not wrestle against flesh and blood, but against the rulers, against the authorities, against the cosmic powers over this present darkness, against the spiritual forces of evil in the heavenly places. Therefore take up the whole armor of God, that you may be able to withstand in the evil day, and having done all, to stand firm. Stand therefore, having fastened on the belt of truth, and having put on the breastplate of righteousness, and, as shoes for your feet, having put on the readiness given by the gospel of peace. In all circumstances take up the shield of faith, with which you can extinguish all the flaming darts of the evil one; and take the helmet of salvation, and the sword of the Spirit, which is the word of God, praying at all times in the Spirit, with all prayer and supplication. To that end keep alert with all perseverance, making supplication for all the saints...

-- Ephesians 6: 10 – 18 (*King James Version*)

Cast of Characters

Simon Reed: Member of psychology department; forties

Thomas: Graduate Assistant to Simon; twenties

Rebecca: Simon's colleague Simon; thirties

Katie: Student; late teens; pretty, athletic

Hardesty: Dean; tall, slender, severe; fifties

Dennis: Priest; short, round; fifties

Scene

The office of Dr. Simon Reed, a university school psychologist. Present day.

ACT I

SCENE ONE

>DR. SIMON REED'S office. A desk sits covered by a mound of books and papers, a bookcase built into the wall behind it. Another desk sits facing out a large window. A few individual chairs are scattered around the room with no rhyme or reason. Above the door is a sign which reads "The Only Source of Knowledge is Experience - Albert Einstein".
>
>THOMAS, a young graduate student enters from an unseen room and takes a seat at the window desk. He sits and spins his chair away from the window to face the office as he begins to read.
>
>DR. SIMON REED enters looking like an academic pack mule, carrying books, papers, and a satchel.

THOMAS
Morning, Dr. Reed....

>(SIMON drops everything as a pile on his desk.)

SIMON
Simon...

THOMAS
Simon...I transcribed your speech notes this weekend. I also updated your October schedule to reflect the Kansas City conference and proofread the one sheet. They had you listed as Reed Simpson.

SIMON
D'oh!

(SIMON looks to THOMAS for some acknowledgement of the joke but gets none. Thomas simply continues his list of deeds.)

SIMON (CONT'D)
Really? Nothing?

THOMAS
I made sure to forward your chapter revisions to the publisher---

SIMON
And happy Monday to you too, Tom.

THOMAS
Thomas...

SIMON
Oh, yes of course.

(Simon is only half listening as he examines what seems to be a piece of inter-office mail. He looks at the envelope as if searching for a clue to its origin. It seems he is surprised to receive something in such a fashion. Before he can open it, Thomas approaches and presents file folders neatly arranged and organized. The contrast between the two is striking.)

THOMAS
I also arranged personnel folders on each of the applicants for next semester's graduate assistants. Dean Hardesty is still expecting a candidate list by the end of this week as well as our weekly appointment evaluations. Then—

SIMON
Then...? Then? Did you work all weekend?

(Thomas sheepishly shrugs his shoulders)

SIMON (CONT'D)
Did you at least go to the grad student happy hour on Friday?

THOMAS
Not much of a drinker.

SIMON
Saturday night date night?

THOMAS
Not much of a dater.

SIMON
And Sunday? Church? Or football? Or something?

THOMAS
I read the Times at Starbucks. Besides, I'm not a big sports fan, and I'm not very superstitious.

SIMON
Superstitious. Now there is a loaded word.

THOMAS
I just meant--

SIMON
Remember, when people come in here, they expect it to be a safe environment where they can talk about any and every thing without fear of retribution or judgment. Our bias -- our personal prejudices - really shouldn't spill into our words. And condescension never should.

THOMAS
I didn't mean--

SIMON
Of course you didn't, but suppose we had a rabbinical student in here because he is having test anxiety over the philosophy class he's auditing. Or one of the sisters from Our Lady of Sorrows who is working on her social work certificate stops by to discuss her conflict at having to counsel a young woman who has just lost a baby...or even killed it?

THOMAS
I just....you know....assumed you were a man of science.

SIMON
I am, but...
(indicating the sign above the doorway)

Like the man said, "The only source of knowledge is experience." And I have not experienced everything. And I have not had my coffee either.
(Simon looks at Thomas expectantly. Thomas pours Simon and cup of coffee and delivers it to his desk.)

Good man. I knew I picked you for a reason.

(Simon takes coffee appreciatively and seems to just let the aroma wash over him as if it is actually helping to awaken him.)

THOMAS
Is it because had you not then you would be perpetually late and rarely in the right place? Because if so, that would make sense...

SIMON
(perusing material from his desk)
While I appreciate the effort you put into keeping my schedule on track, I did somehow manage before you graced me with your time.

THOMAS
Don't you have a grad assistant every semester?

SIMON
(still reading)
I do.

THOMAS
And aren't they in charge of your schedule?

SIMON
They are.

THOMAS
So when was the last time you were in charge of your own schedule?

SIMON
Oh, probably seven years ago.

THOMAS
Isn't that when you got married?

SIMON
(stops reading)
Now you're catching on.

(SIMON resumes browsing mail and reading.)

THOMAS
(now busy with his own work at his own desk)
Wasn't your wife your assistant before you got married?

SIMON
She was indeed. A good while before. Four or five years. And just like you, she had her own case load and her own clients. In fact until we were expecting, her practice was thriving. Just as, I am certain, one day yours will be as well.

THOMAS
So she gave up her practice to have a baby? That isn't very progressive.

SIMON
Nor is it for what either of us had hoped. However, her pregnancy turned out to be high-risk -- one of life's little curve balls -- so we opted to preserve her safety rather than worrying whether or not she would disappoint "progressives".

THOMAS
You say that like it's an antagonistic relationship. In theory isn't progress a good thing? And there were options that didn't involve rolling the dice with your wife's health.

SIMON
(Carefully considering what is
not being spoken)

Rolling the dice?

Such as?

THOMAS

Well, you know--

SIMON
(prodding)

No. I don't. Explain.

THOMAS
(unsure but fairly certain he is
being led into a trick bag)

Uh, I was just meaning that if a woman doesn't want to go through with a pregnancy, she has a choice to go other directions.

SIMON
(toying with him)

Like adoption?

THOMAS

Well, no. I mean that would essentially cause the same problem.

SIMON

So not adoption?

THOMAS

Dr. Reed, why are doing this? You know what I mean. Surely you can't be such a zealot that you are willing to forego the safety of a loved one. That defies common sense.

SIMON

Does it? Hmm. Let me address two important points you bring up. First and foremost, our job as psychologists -- albeit in your case, one in training -- is to listen. It isn't to mold or shape them. It is not to judge. And it most certainly is not to condemn. Our patients are looking for comfort, for insight, for...some degree of understanding. How will they ever achieve any of that if our responses attempt to put them on the defensive?

THOMAS

I was simply saying...

SIMON
Exactly. You should be simply listening. And secondly, never, but never, make the mistake of believing that our theories and personal predispositions exist in a vacuum. The patients' experiences, their value systems -- these things feed into their stories. Stories they are trying to tell us.

THOMAS
Of course I know that.

SIMON
You do?

THOMAS
I just think they are best served if we have responses for them. They aren't paying to talk to a wall. We need to say something.

SIMON
Really? So tell me, what would you say to a patient who comes to you having lost two children in utero only to find herself facing a third pregnancy that, in all likelihood, will not come to term? What do you say to her when she tells you the only thing she wants in this world is to have a child no matter what personal risks she faces? What would you say to her? Would you tell her to consider her options?

THOMAS
Maybe, I don't...

SIMON
What precisely would you suggest to her?

> (Beat. THOMAS seems at a loss for words. SIMON senses that perhaps he has taken this a bit too personally and tries to real the conversation back to a less contentious level)

Everyone has a story. It is our job to listen to them.

THOMAS
Is that what happened with your wife?

SIMON
(pauses reflectively)
Yes. Yes it is.

                    THOMAS
I'm sorry, Dr. Simon, I didn't know.

                    SIMON
That's alright. But, again, this is a conversation between colleagues so you get a little leeway with the condescension...

                    THOMAS
              (trying to talk over SIMON)
I wasn't condescending...

                    SIMON (CONT'D)
              (continuing without interruption)
...that in a therapeutic setting could create a substantial chasm...

                    THOMAS (CONT'D)
              (They are now talking over one
                another.)
..at least I didn't think I was. I was just surprised because...you just don't very often find someone so I don't know, conventional I guess, in...

                    SIMON (CONT'D)
              (continuing to make his point)
...Remember, making someone feel comfortable is more than a skill and more than even an art. It is a...

                    BOTH
              (in unison)
...Science

              (SIMON and THOMAS simply
                stare at each other somewhat
                bemused by the fact that they
                both ended up at essentially
                the same spot in their
                argument. THOMAS tries not to
                wilt under SIMON'S gaze but
                eventually gives up and returns
                to his desk. SIMON follows
                suit)

                    THOMAS
So how did she keep you on track?

                    SIMON
Who?

THOMAS
Your wife. When she was your graduate assistant, what was her secret for keeping you on track.

SIMON
Oh, much the same as now. She'd fill in my calendar, point me where I needed to be, and gently shove me along.

THOMAS
Kind of like me?

SIMON
Her touch was a bit softer...and infinitely more appealing.

THOMAS
Obviously.

SIMON
Don't worry Thomas, marrying me is not in your job description nor will your obvious aversion to the thought affect your grade Just keep treating your cases with the same professional touch and supplying your keen insight and all will be well.

THOMAS
(sneezes)
Excuse me.

SIMON
(without looking up)
God bless you.

(THOMAS says nothing. SIMON notices this and looks at him pointedly.)

You're welcome.

(SIMON lifts his coffee and briefly seems to be entranced by its aroma)

THOMAS
So, since there are no rabbis or nuns in here at the moment, may I ask you a personal question.

SIMON
Sure.

THOMAS
Are you? You know? Superstitious?

(Somewhat surprised by the question, SIMON'S caffeine trance now appears to be broken as he considers.)

SIMON
Wow. You weren't kidding. That was personal.

THOMAS
I'm sorry. I just thought--

SIMON
No...no, no, no. Totally fair question. Um....If You are asking me if I am a person of faith...Yes....

THOMAS
Which faith?

SIMON
Christian. Raised Catholic...if you are asking me if I am an ardent church-goer...sometimes.

THOMAS
Oh yeah? When?

SIMON
I am, what has often been referred to as a "C and E Catholic".

THOMAS
(shaking his head in confusion)
C and E?

SIMON
Christmas and Easter. You know, the big holidays. You go with family. You have dinner. You argue politics or sports. And then you go home to recover until the next one.

THOMAS
So no road to Damascus moment as they say? No circumstance or big event that solidified your belief system.

SIMON

Not that I can remember.

(He stops to think)

No. I guess not.

THOMAS

You just kind of always believed then.

SIMON
(thoughtfully)

I...guess so.

THOMAS

If you'll excuse me for saying so Dr.....Simon....it seems that your idea of being a person faith and the traditional notion are a bit far apart.

SIMON

How do you mean?

THOMAS

Well, from my arguably limited exposure to people "of faith", as you put it, it seems that those who profess to take their faith seriously...

SIMON
(overlapping)

Profess? Am I hearing bias again?

THOMAS
(undaunted)

They seem to at least go through the standard motions of daily or weekly worship, prayer, studying scripture.

SIMON

And?

THOMAS

And, it just seems that you don't strike me as a particularly prayerful kind of person.

SIMON

Prayer is personal endeavor.

THOMAS
Agreed. I didn't mean to offend. It's just that I find it hard to reconcile your science and your superstition.

SIMON
Faith.

THOMAS
Sorry. Faith. I mean they do seem to be rather at odds, wouldn't you agree?

SIMON
No. Not at all. I have heard the idea that faith tries to fill in for our lack of understanding, a "God of the gaps" kind of thing. But science and religion are not polar opposites. They needn't be considered antagonistic.

THOMAS
Tell that to Galileo.

SIMON
Different time, different place, different knowledge, different rules.

THOMAS
Doesn't that kind of explain it then?

SIMON
What?

THOMAS
Different knowledge.

SIMON
No. Not really. It is just. Knowledge is the sum of all we have learned and know.

THOMAS
In other words, science.

SIMON
Not necessarily. I mean science is provable and repeatable. At least, it's supposed to be right? That's where people start to diverge and get into what usually amount to semantic battles. Faith, now that is a horse of a different color. A very grey, very subjective color. It is essentially belief in that which cannot be definitively proven. If it could, then, by definition it would--

THOMAS
No longer be faith. I get it. Still, I am always skeptical when scientists start depending upon their faith. I feel they have compromised themselves somewhat at that point. But I guess I really don't have to worry too much in this case, huh?

SIMON
Meaning?

THOMAS
Nothing. It's just that I think an actual person of faith would at least go to church more than twice a year...

> (Simon has returned his attention to the inter-office mail envelope and its contents. He is still talking but obviously engrossed in whatever it is that he is reading.)

SIMON
That's the thing with going to parochial school all your life. You go to church two or three times a week, and you tend to think as if you have banked all this time. Like, you have some kind of quota to fill and you're getting ahead of the game so later in life if you miss a week or two or 102, you kind of figure that you're still even.

> (He holds up an envelope and the sheet he has pulled from within.)

Did you bring me this?

THOMAS
No it was on your desk this morning.

> (Simon reaches for the phone, and is preparing to dial as there is a knock on the office door followed quickly by its opening. REBECCA, a friend and colleague strides into the room.)

SIMON
Rebecca. I was just calling you.

REBECCA
I kind of figured you'd be calling so I thought I'd save you the dial. Morning Tom.

THOMAS
Good morning Professor Collins.
(good-naturedly)
And, uh, actually ma'am, it's Thomas.

(His correction has stopped her in her tracks. She wheels back around to Simon bemused by the fact that she seems to have inadvertently offended the young man who has disappeared into the back room.)

SIMON
Yeah, I got that too. He seems to have a thing about name clipping. At least he smiles at you.

REBECCA
Trouble in paradise?

SIMON
No. I just don't think he likes me very much. He's such a serious young man.

REBECCA
So he has a stick up his...

SIMON
(interrupting)
He's a serious young man. Coffee?

REBECCA
Bless you.

(Simon pours her a cup and mixes in sugar and cream. It is apparent that he knows the routine.)

That's the problem with these grad assistants. They all seem to be so caught up in the idea of teaching that they forget the joy of it.

18

SIMON
(returning with coffee)

The joy of it?

REBECCA

Well, the purported joy of it. Thanks.

SIMON

So you rather they find out about the dark side of the vocation in their own time.

REBECCA

Heck yeah. Like we had to. With endless memos, countless meetings, and useless evaluations. Not to mention publish or perish.

SIMON
(raising his cup in a faux toast)

To deans and deadlines.

REBECCA
(returning the favor)

To whining students and excuses.

SIMON

State schools.

REBECCA

State standards.

SIMON

Tenure.

BOTH
(completing their toast in earnest)

To higher education.

(Simon returns to his seat behind his desk and holds up the envelope in question once again.)

SIMON

So?

19

REBECCA
Ah yes, Miss Katie.

SIMON
(selectively reading information aloud)
Katelyn McCarthy. 19. 3rd semester freshman...Believes In taking her time does she?

REBECCA
Not necessarily. She has had some unusual circumstances.

SIMON
(still engrossed in his reading)
Like what?

(It dawns on her he hasn't yet read that which she has sent him.)

REBECCA
I am so sorry, Simon. I just assumed you had read that already. I sent it over Friday morning.

SIMON
Took Friday off. Elizabeth had an ultrasound.

REBECCA
And...?

SIMON
Still no change. I mean, you know, they're hopeful. As long as we don't hear anything back from the last round of tests...

REBECCA
No news is good news.

SIMON
Basically. It's exhausting.

REBECCA
I bet. How is Liz holding up?

SIMON
Fine. She's pretty strong that way.

REBECCA

Boy or girl?

SIMON
(back to reading)
Don't know. We don't want to know. One of the few surprises left. I don't even know this baby's gender yet, but I can tell you the number of platelets she has or his white blood cell count. They insist on culling every possible bit of data they can.

REBECCA

The devil's in the details.

(Simon smiles at her turn of
phrase and walks back around
his desk pulling a chair up
alongside hers.)

SIMON

So it would seem. Is this really suggesting what I think it is?
(Rebecca nods mischievously.)

REBECCA

I thought you'd get a kick out of this.

(He looks at her as if to see if
she is going to smile or betray
that this is a joke of some
sort.)

SIMON

You're serious?

REBECCA

As a heart attack.

SIMON
(reading aloud from the report)
Subject illustrates clear mental and emotional distress manifesting in physical trauma, psychotic outbursts, as well as a series of audible phenomena. Additionally, subject has been observed positioning her body in a variety of improbable contortions and speaking a language reportedly unrecognizable to her in a non-distressed state. While these may all be attributed to any of a series of neurological or physiological conditions, the subject fears she is suffering from demonic possession.

(Simon looks to Rebecca, again
as if expecting her to admit
that this is a joke of some
sort.)

REBECCA
Cool, huh?

SIMON
No. It's not cool. It's some girl desperately seeking attention at best or suffering some serious mental crisis at worse.

REBECCA
I know. I just mean how often do you get to say that you will be treating someone who's possessed?

SIMON
Including today? Never. I am a little out of my depth on this one. You need to get someone who specializes.

REBECCA
Do you suggest I call the Vatican?

SIMON
No.
(Returning behind his desk, he
begins to jot something on a
piece of paper)
But I do suggest you give this gentleman a call.
(He hands the paper to her.)

REBECCA
Steven Engler.

SIMON
Director of Psychiatric Medicine at St. John's.

REBECCA
Sorry, but no can do.

SIMON
Why not?

REBECCA
School wants to keep this one in-house. Publicity on this could kill us for years.

SIMON
From what? You don't honestly believe...

(She shrugs her shoulders as if to say "Who knows"?)

Come on. You know that this is probably--

REBECCA
Even so...the university wants this quietly addressed.

SIMON
By me?

REBECCA
That's right, Mr. School Psychologist. That there title is what gets you this fancy office and that big ol' desk. And it gets you the pleasure of navigating a sea of difficult cases among the student body.

SIMON
(shaking his head in disbelief)
This is unbelievable. Are they serious? The school wants to dedicate resources to this?

REBECCA
Well, she needs help.

SIMON
(reading again)
Clearly.

REBECCA
And she is a student. Still, I am relatively sure their desire to help is less motivated by concern for her well-being and more so for fear of a law suit.

SIMON
What do you mean?

REBECCA
You really haven't read this.

SIMON
I'm trying.

REBECCA
Put that down. I'll fill you in on the rest.

SIMON
There's more?

REBECCA
Much.

>   (Simon crosses to the front of
>   his desk and leans on it placing
>   the folder down.)

Apparently, it goes back to her freshman year...her first freshman year. It began with little things -- sleepwalking, night terrors, talking in her sleep. It got so bad her dorm-mate took to sleeping on a couch in the RA's office.

SIMON
And that's when you got involved.

>   (Thomas has re-entered and
>   takes a seat at his tiny desk by
>   the window. He begins to
>   work, but the conversation
>   slowly draws his interest, and
>   he listens.)

REBECCA
Right. As the Dorm Advisor, I was asked to come in and make sure there wasn't more to the situation. My RA and I talked to the girl, and she assured us that Katie was basically a fine roommate but this particular girl was a basketball player and needed her rest. Between a full-course load and practice and work, she was perpetually spent. We all agreed to talk to Katie.

SIMON
And Katie was oblivious to all the activity?

REBECCA
Not only that, she seemed genuinely surprised and more than a little upset. Anyway, she and the roommate agreed to take

REBECCA (CONT'D)
another go at things. After a couple of days, the roommate asked to go somewhere else.

SIMON
Another room?

REBECCA
Another college.

THOMAS
A little drastic.

REBECCA
(surprised by his input)
That's what we thought until the new roommate showed up.

(Thomas, realizing he may have overstepped, turns quickly around and pretends to read, but he is clearly still listening.)

Another basketball player, good student, work-study. Same deal, by and large. Very active in campus ministry. The first night she got the full show -- sleepwalking, talking, and terrors. But this time around a new trick was added to the show. Girl claims in the morning while she was dressing for class, a book flew off the shelf and hit her. And not in the back. Says it hit her square in the chest. She watched it happen.

SIMON
Where was Katie?

REBECCA
In bed. Watching. Smiling. The other girl was so upset that she ran out of the room without even finishing getting dressed. She lasted less than 24 hours. When Katie finally heard the story, she broke down in tears and went to the school med center.

SIMON
So where did the "possession" stuff come from?

REBECCA
We think the second roommate probably said something and that got picked up by someone who told someone who told someone. And the rest is history.

SIMON
(He is again browsing through
the file.)
And lurid campus legend.

REBECCA
It didn't help that the first roommate had basically scrambled off of campus less than two weeks into the semester.

SIMON
Did it ever occur to you that she got exactly what she wanted?

REBECCA
Who?

SIMON
Katie.

REBECCA
How so?

SIMON
She got a dorm suite all to herself. I mean I used to order anchovy pizzas just to get my college roommate to leave the room.

REBECCA
Yeah, that crossed my mind. Except that she has pleaded with us to find her a new roommate. Poor kid is so freaked about the stories she doesn't want to be alone in the room. In fact, she has started spending the night on the RA's couch.

SIMON
So who did this work-up? Has she been seeing someone?

REBECCA
The family sent someone, but apparently he was less convinced than you.

SIMON
And I am nowhere near convinced. In fact I am positively un-convinced.

REBECCA
Exactly. Look, space is at a premium. If we can fill that room, we need too. And if we can't do that with Katie there, then we will

REBECCA (CONT'D)
have to move her and do it without. But, we have to make certain that she won't be in danger by herself.

SIMON
From what? The boogey man?

REBECCA
From herself...or the boogey man.

SIMON
You believe the stories.

REBECCA
I don't know what I believe. I do know, though, that I trust your opinion, and the university wants this to happen.

SIMON
Alright. Talk to Thomas. We'll set something up. Have her stop by my office tomorrow or Wednesday...

REBECCA
She'll be here this afternoon.

SIMON
What?

REBECCA
After lunch. The university wants this handled quietly...and quickly.

SIMON
Alright. I will talk to the scary girl.

REBECCA
Be nice. Besides, this could make for a heck of a case study for that journal whose pages you seem to covet so dearly.

SIMON
Sounds better suited to the *Twilight Zone*.

REBECCA
Whichever.
    (She starts toward the door.)

SIMON
Hey! Did Elizabeth ever get a hold of you?

REBECCA
Yes. And, yes, I would love to be godmother to him...or her...
> (She looks for a reaction. He gives none)

So which is it?

SIMON
We're not saying.

REBECCA
So you do know! Name?

SIMON
(purposefully coy)
Yeah. We've picked one.

REBECCA
Come on. Not even for a Godmother-in-waiting?

SIMON
Nope.

REBECCA
Fine. Be that way.
> (She makes her way toward the door, stops, and twirls toward him.)

How about a hint?

SIMON
(with mock sternness)
No.

REBECCA
Why you ornery little cuss. I'll just ask Liz.

SIMON
She's not talking either.

REBECCA
Yeah, well you'll be here, and she'll be home all alone. Never underestimate a plate of brownies waved under a pregnant

                    REBECCA (CONT'D)
woman's nose. I'll call you later tonight to see how it went. And,
Simon, be careful.
                              (REBECCA leaves. THOMAS has
                              fully turned around in his seat
                              and is staring at SIMON who
                              seems at a loss for words. He
                              simply shrugs his shoulders.)

                    SIMON
Maybe this will make a good article after all...
                              (THOMAS shakes his head in a
                              mixture of amazement and
                              disapproval. FADE TO BLACK.)

SCENE TWO

> It is considerably later in the day. THOMAS is straightening up, and occasionally runs the odd paper or file over to SIMON'S desk. He begins filling in dates on the wall calendar.
>
> Simon comes in and begins to "smarten up" -- rolling down and buttoning his sleeves, tightening his tie, and slipping into his coat.
>
> He pulls a file, probably the case in question and scans it thoroughly.

THOMAS

The weekend of the 18th is double-booked. Would you rather drop the Columbia conference or the M-APA consortium in Springfield?

SIMON

Which is which?

THOMAS

Columbia is presenting your paper on the Hanson project, and you are an honorary chair of the AP Psych panel in Springfield.

SIMON
(barely paying attention)

Columbia.

THOMAS
(beginning to erase)

OK, the paper it is.

SIMON
(realizing he may have committed without paying attention)

Wait, no, Springfield gets me home on Saturday?

(As THOMAS is busy at the calendar and SIMON is engrossed in the file, KATIE, young, fresh-faced, and decidedly feminine walks in unnoticed. She is dressed like a typical student in jeans and a baggy sweater.)

THOMAS
I'm not sure, maybe. I can call--

SIMON
(reconsidering his own hesitation)
Wait, no, never mind. Just find out if there is a game in Columbia that weekend.

THOMAS
There isn't.

SIMON
How do you know?

THOMAS
My brother is in the band. They are at College-Station. Texas.

SIMON
Oh. Well they still have Shakespeare's Pizza.
(He thoughtfully considers for a moment.)
Tie goes to the pizza.

THOMAS
You sure?

SIMON
Yes...for now.

THOMAS
I can't believe you are basing your calendar on pizza.

KATIE
Spoken like a man who has never had Shakespeare's.

> (Both THOMAS and SIMON turn to see KATIE standing un-assumingly near the middle of the room. THOMAS begins finishing a few odds and ends but is obviously interested in the young lady -- not like most guys would be but rather like an experiment of some sort.)

SIMON
Katie?

KATIE
Yes, sir.

SIMON
Welcome. I'm Dr. Reed.
> (He extends his hand and ushers her near to the chairs)

This is my assistant, Thomas.
> (She waves cautiously to THOMAS who is still staring)

I appreciate your stopping by today.

KATIE
No problem. I appreciate you taking the time to talk to me.

SIMON
Well, Professor Collins mentioned that this might be kind of an...urgent situation.

KATIE
Yeah.
> (She shyly looks in the direction of THOMAS)

About that...

SIMON
Just a second. Thomas, I think we're good today.

THOMAS

> (snapping out of his momentary fixation and quickly jotting and posting notes on the calendar)

Yes. I've got just the last week to confirm and--

SIMON
> (pointedly)

Thomas...We're good.
> (THOMAS has stopped and seems unsure what to do if he is not to finish. SIMON gives THOMAS a firm but patient look).

You got through a lot today. Thanks.

THOMAS

Right. Right. You're welcome.
> (puts on a jacket and grabs his pack)

I can just, you know, finish that tomorrow.

SIMON

Excellent.
> (THOMAS places a final folder on SIMON'S desk and in the process finds himself passing KATIE on his way out)

THOMAS

Nice to meet you.
> (He extends his hand to KATIE as if to shake, but her hesitancy and his backpack sliding off of his shoulder instead cause an awkward interaction which leads to him bolting out the door.)

KATIE

You too.
> (She is still a bit unnerved by the weird exchange.)

I guess I shouldn't expect people to feel comfortable around "The Haunted Girl".

SIMON
Oh, I wish I could claim it was just you, but he is pretty much like that with everyone.

KATIE
Slim pickings in the grad school this year, huh?

SIMON
You have no idea. But, at least he can alphabetize which is more than I can say for my last assistant. You never appreciate basic skills until they're absent.

KATIE
Like filing?

SIMON
Like knowing the alphabet in the first place. Please sit.

(They both sit.)

So, do you really think you're "haunted"?

KATIE
So they say.

SIMON
And what do you say?

KATIE
I say that apparently I won't be getting a lot of roommate requests.

SIMON
Yes. Professor Collins mentioned your run of bad luck in that department.

KATIE
Bad luck? Bad luck is getting to the cafeteria after 6 on pudding night or finally meeting the hot guy from Biology Lab on the day you decide to sleep late and skip showering. Bad luck is not walking around your dorm room speaking in tongues or objects flying off shelves.

SIMON
And what do you call that?

                    KATIE
                  (pause)
Scary.

                    SIMON
I don't find you scary at all.

                    KATIE
Stick around.
                  (Perhaps to put her at ease,
                   perhaps because he is startled
                   by the response, SIMON leans
                   back in his chair.)

                    SIMON
What can you tell me about yourself?

                    KATIE
Other than the fact that I probably won't be invited to any slumber parties any time soon?

                    SIMON
Yeah. Other than that.

                    KATIE
Sorry, but it's going to be pretty boring I'm afraid. Mom and dad still married. 25 years. Older brother Danny in the Marines, deployed overseas and still threatening to break any guy in half that even looks at me. Little sister. Sophomore. Learning to drive and date. She's happy when I come home, but happier when I am at school so she can wear all the stuff that I can't squeeze into my closet here.

                    SIMON
Pretty typical.

                    KATIE
Pretty typical.

                    SIMON
How are your classes?

                    KATIE
Pretty good. Not honor roll good, but, you know, pretty good.

SIMON
What are taking this semester?

KATIE
Full load. Comp. Biology.

(SIMON nods attentively.)
General Psych.

SIMON
Nice.

KATIE
Thought you'd like that one...Comparative Religions--

SIMON
(interrupting)
Tell me about that one.

KATIE
Comparative Religions? Um...not much to tell. We take these different religions...and...um, compare them?

SIMON
OK, that much I got. Do you like the class?

KATIE
It's okay I guess.

SIMON
You guess?

KATIE
Yeah. I mean there is a lot of reading so far. I mean a lot. I don't mind reading something if I am interested in it but...

SIMON
Religion doesn't interest you?

KATIE
Not really. Not as much as Biology.

SIMON
Biology interests you or the cute boy in Biology interests you?

KATIE
(smiles, somewhat
embarrassed)

Guilty.

SIMON

Let's talk a little more about your Comparative Religions class. That's...who is that? Lawrence?

KATIE

Uh huh.

SIMON

Was that a class you wanted to take? I can't imagine you needed to.

KATIE

It was an elective. I needed one.

SIMON

There are a lot of electives.

KATIE

I don't know. It seemed interesting I guess. I was wrong. But initially....

SIMON

Are you a religious person? Do you attend services? Were you raised in a family of believers?

KATIE

Not overly so. I mean I was baptized. I went to St. Elizabeth's High School. We go to church ...kind of...

SIMON

...on Christmas and Easter.

(Katie seems genuinely
surprised.)

KATIE

Yeah. How did you know?

SIMON

A lot of that going around.

KATIE
Weird.

(KATIE jumps up unexpectedly.
SIMON is somewhat taken
aback.)

Hey can I walk around a little? Is that allowed?

SIMON
Sure.

KATIE
Thanks. I'm not used to sitting down a lot. Class is tough enough.

(as if she has just heard that
phrase for the first time)

Class is tough enough.

SIMON
Let me guess, an athlete.

KATIE
Yep. Eight years gymnastics, four years cheer leading, and a couple more competitive dance.

SIMON
Still?

KATIE
(She has wandered over to the
desk by the window and is
staring out as she seems to
limber up a bit, perhaps
unconsciously.)

Nah. No time really. I still work out and do a little yoga, but now it's mostly class. Especially this semester. I have some credits to make up. I'll have to take a few extra classes in spring and summer just to get back on track for junior year.

SIMON
And this is because you missed last semester?

KATIE
And a good chunk of the semester before.

(She makes her way around the
back of SIMON'S desk, hands
in pockets and scanning books
on the shelf)

I had to drop most of my classes. Couldn't keep up. Too much work. Too little sleep.

(almost examining the words as
she says them)

...too...little...sleep.

SIMON

I imagine that can take its toll.

(KATIE makes her way back
toward the window. She stands
looking out.)

Well, now you're back and at a full load.

KATIE

Mm-hmm.

(On the bookshelf, a single
book falls over onto its spine
causing a loud noise that
startles SIMON. However,
KATIE is unmoved.)

SIMON
(laughing somewhat nervously)

That...that was unusual.

KATIE
(Her voice slightly less perky as
it has been previously)

Not as much as you'd think.

(SIMON takes it in stride as he
wanders to the bookcase. He
picks up the book that has
fallen over and examines it. He
smiles as he holds it up. KATIE
turns to him.)

SIMON

Hmm.

KATIE

What?

SIMON

The book.
(reading the title)

"The Dark Side of Me" by David Scott. Good resource. But look, I've never even creased the spine.

KATIE

I bet that's about to change.

(BLACKOUT)

SCENE THREE

> THOMAS, holding a text book at which he glances periodically, is seated upright in his desk chair which is placed directly across the room from SIMON who is reclined and casually tossing a racquet ball in the air from time to time. This seems to be less recreational and more meditative for him.

SIMON

Dissociative amnesia.

THOMAS
(reading)

Schizophrenia.

SIMON

Depersonalization disorder.

THOMAS
(still reading)

Borderline personality disorder.

SIMON

Dissociative fugue.

THOMAS
(again depending on the book
 for his part in the
 conversation)

Um...Malingering.

SIMON
(He has stopped tossing the ball
 upward and holds it
 contemplatively.)

Possession.

                    THOMAS
              (He has stopped reading and
               looks in shock at SIMON who
               stares somberly at him.)
What?!?
              (Beat. SIMON breaks into a wide
               grin signaling to THOMAS that
               he was merely kidding.)
Thank God.

                    SIMON
              (teasing)
Now who's superstitious?

                    THOMAS
              (defensively)
You know what I mean!

                    SIMON
Yes, Thomas, I know what you mean. And, to put your mind at ease, let me tell you directly that I do not believe that young Miss Katie is any more possessed than you or I.

                    THOMAS
              (visibly relieved)
Dr. Simon, you really had me worried.

                    SIMON
Did I? Not looking forward to taking on the Great Deceiver were you?

                    THOMAS
We still might be. Albeit, not the Biblical character.

                    SIMON
Yeah. I had thought of that. It certainly would explain some of the more dramatic touches...

              (SIMON seems to have
               stumbled onto something
               that has piqued his interest)

When you're at the administrative offices later, stop by the registrar and get a copy of Katie's application, her high school records, and the transcripts from her first two semesters. Just give them my ID number if they ask.

                    THOMAS
Okay. What are you going to be looking for?

                    SIMON
I just want to check for an element I may have been overlooking.

                    THOMAS
Oh. And when am I supposed to be going to the admin offices?

                    SIMON
Any time now. I requested the family medical records be couriered over. Since they rarely make it to my office directly, packages generally get hung up in the mail room and...

                (The telephone rings.)

...they call.
                (THOMAS stands as SIMON
                  speaks into the phone.)
Simon.
                (Beat, as THOMAS has
                  started toward the door.)
OK. Great.
                (SIMON signals that the
                  records are ready.)

I am sending my assistant right over. Mm Hmm. Thanks.
                (As THOMAS exits, DEAN
                  HARDESTY, 60ish and severe
                  looking enters and waits for
                  SIMON to finish his call.)

He's on his way. Alright.

                    HARDESTY
Busy day?

                    SIMON
                (hanging up)
Oh you know, the usual. Eating disorders. Home sickness. Demonic possession...

				HARDESTY

Actually, Simon, that's why I'm here. I was hoping you could give me an update on where...the situation...stands.

				SIMON

Well, nothing conclusive yet. I've just sent for the complete family medical history. That should fill in some background on conditions or diagnoses with which we may be contending. I have met with the young lady once already. She will be coming by again today. Very respectful. Very bright. I suspect that if she is capable, she will share.

				HARDESTY

What do you mean by "capable"?

				SIMON

If her, currently unlabeled, condition allows.

				HARDESTY

Any preliminary thoughts on what "label" you might ascribe?

				SIMON

Multiple mannerisms, time distortion, derealization, memory loss, auditory distortion. Realistically we are looking at a dissociative disorder. We're just not sure which one.

				HARDESTY

And unrealistically?

				SIMON

Boo.

				HARDESTY
				(smiles uncomfortably)

Simon, I don't have to tell you how a situation like this can spiral out of control. It's got to be handled quickly...

				SIMON

..and quietly. I know. Franklin, just give me a couple of days. The family history should yield something, and if not, the girl herself will, I am sure, give up the ghost. So to speak.

				HARDESTY

Thank you, Simon. That means a lot.

				(pointedly)

HARDESTY (CONT'D)
You have a growing family. A bright future. I'd truly hate for this episode to reflect negatively on the university...or any member of the faculty.

    (He makes his way toward the door which quickly opens as THOMAS returns with a fairly large box.)

THOMAS
Here are the medical files, Simon. Oh good morning, Dean Hardesty.

    (He sets them on SIMON'S desk.)

HARDESTY
    (leaving)
Good morning, Thomas.

SIMON
I didn't know you knew the dean.

THOMAS
Oh yeah, kind of. He is looking over a grant proposal I am submitting for next semester.

SIMON
He's a good person to have in your corner.

THOMAS
Yeah. I'd sure hate to be on the wrong side of him. Wouldn't you?

    (SIMON ignores the question and walks back behind his desk where he opens the box and removes stacks and stacks of file folders.)

SIMON
Looks like I have some lunch time reading ahead of me.

THOMAS
Just a little. What are you looking for?

SIMON
(randomly flipping through
folders until he picks up one of
particular interest)
I am not really certain. I guess anything that helps us fill in the blanks with anything that may have colored her past.

(He puts all but one folder down
and reads intently.)

Thomas, how did she describe the composition of her family?

THOMAS
Mom and dad married for a long time. Brother in Iraq. Little sister in high school.

SIMON
Huh.

THOMAS
What did you find?

SIMON
Maybe a color. A very bright, very primary color.

(FADE TO BLACK)

SCENE FOUR

> The office is still. KATIE, dressed in workout pants and a hooded sweatshirt, enters and casually strolls around awaiting the arrival of SIMON. She looks briefly out the window, breezes behind his desk careful not to look at anything that might be none of her business. She then stops at the bookcases and peruses the titles. SIMON comes out of the back room drying his hands on a paper towel.

SIMON
Oh, Katie, are you early?

KATIE
(checking her cell phone)
I don't think so.

SIMON
(looking over his shoulder at his
wall calendar)
Oh, nope, I'm late. Sorry. Please, please. Sit down. It has been quite a day.

KATIE
Well, it's been a long one.

SIMON
Didn't sleep?

KATIE
Apparently not.
(SIMON looks confused)
They didn't contact you, yet?

SIMON
Who?

KATIE
The RA, campus security, Professor Collins.

SIMON
No, why?

KATIE
It seems I had a pretty active night.

SIMON
What happened?

KATIE
I don't really know. I remember laying down on the couch in Jennifer the RA's room. She was going in to take a shower, and I was trying to go to sleep. Then...

SIMON
Yes?

KATIE
That's just it. I don't know. I don't remember anything after trying to fall asleep. She says that after she got out of the shower she heard noises coming from the room so she walked in and...

SIMON
Go on, Katie.

KATIE
(in an almost-hushed tone)
Go on Katie. Katie, go on.

SIMON
Katie?
(KATIE looks momentarily lost
and then continues)

KATIE
She says that I was trying to crawl up the wall.

SIMON
Crawl...?

KATIE
...up the wall. Yeah. I know. It sounds crazy, right. But no more than any of this other stuff going on.

SIMON
No one has said anything to me yet?

                              KATIE

They will.
                    (again in an almost hushed tone
                     as if to an unseen audience)

They will.

                    (SIMON gets up and pours
                     KATIE a glass of water. She
                     makes her way to the far desk
                     and stares out the window for
                     a moment.)

                              SIMON

There. Let's...let's try to gather ourselves here and pick up from
where we were last time.

                    (returning to his seat)

We were talking about Comparative Religions with Lawrence.

                              KATIE
                    (still staring out the window)

We were...?

                              SIMON

I thought...

                    (As SIMON consults his notes,
                     he does not notice that KATIE
                     has removed her hoodie and is
                     now wearing only a sports bra.
                     She undoes her hair from the
                     band in which it had been
                     tied.)

Yes. We were.

                              KATIE

No. You were talking. I was listening.

                              SIMON

I'm sorry. Did you want to talk about something else? I just
thought--

KATIE
(Her voice now has a sing-song,
almost childlike quality to it
that almost seems to echo.)
Something else....something else...something else...

SIMON
Well, there is a little "something else" I'd like to discuss. You mentioned your family--

KATIE
Let's-talk-about-the-fa-mi-ly...

SIMON
You mentioned your parents having been together for 25 years.

KATIE
(overly sweetly)
Such love and devotion.

SIMON
...and you mentioned your brother in Iraq.

KATIE
(with mock pride)
A defender of the faith....Yay!

SIMON
...and a little sister--

KATIE
(with mild disdain)
So special to me. So very special.

SIMON
But you never mentioned...

KATIE
He's going to ask. He's going to. Do you think he'll ask? I hope he asks. I hope so.

SIMON
(SIMON turns and sees KATIE
has removed her sweatshirt
and let her hair fall)
Katie?

(He starts to approach
cautiously.)

KATIE
(Her voice has taken on the air
of a chorus, almost as if many
people are speaking at once
and in rounds.)
Katie. Katie. Katie.

(SIMON slowly takes his cell
phone out of his pocket. And
dials, trying to keep his eyes
on KATIE the entire time.)

SIMON
(into the phone)
Thomas, please come back to the office. I need your help. Yes. Thank you.

(KATIE has taken up residency
atop the desk and is perching
like a bird of prey.)

Katie? Please take a seat.

KATIE
Ask me nicely.

SIMON
Katie, please--

KATIE
No! Ask ME nicely.

SIMON
And you would be...?

KATIE
Sshhhhh. No clues. No clues. No clues. He wants to know. He wants to know. Sshhhhh.

(For a brief second KATIE
adopts her own voice once
more and outstretches her
arms as if pleading.)

Dr. Reed!

SIMON

Katie?

(KATIE jumps off of the desk
and leans against the desk.)

KATIE
(singing)

K-K-K-Katie, beautiful Katie. You're the only g-g-g-girl that I adore.

(She begins twirling in a sort of
a dance finally finishing the
song seated in her chair.)

When the m-m-m-moonshines over the cowshed, I'll be waiting at the k-k-k-kitchen door.

(She strikes a somewhat
provocative pose.)

You like?

SIMON

Katie. Please.

(At that moment THOMAS
knocks.)

THOMAS
(offstage)

Dr. Reed?

(Both SIMON and KATIE look
toward the door.)

SIMON

Thomas, come in.

(KATIE quickly snaps her head
around.)

KATIE
(in what amounts to a hiss)

She's going away.

(KATIE slumps as if all the air
has rushed out of her body. At
that moment THOMAS rushes
in accompanied by REBECCA.)

SIMON
(kneeling beside KATIE who
appears to be out)

Rebecca?

52

                    REBECCA
            (joining him beside her)
I was heading for my car and ran into Thomas. He sounded...

                    THOMAS
Unnerved?

                    SIMON
            (gathering up the sweatshirt and
            handing it to REBECCA)
Join the club. Katie. Katie?

            (KATIE seems to be coming
            around.)

                    KATIE
Dr. Reed...

            (KATIE is at a loss for words.
            SIMON simply nods.)

                    SIMON
Rebecca, can you..?

                    REBECCA
Of course.

            (REBECCA places the sweatshirt
            around KATIE'S shoulders and
            helps her out of the chair.)
Come on, sweetheart....

            (REBECCA leads her out. KATIE
            appears to be genuinely
            confused and disoriented.)

                    THOMAS
What happened?

                    SIMON
            (Surveying the scene as if
            replaying it moment by
            moment.)
I don't know quite how to explain it...yet.

THOMAS
So she's not...

SIMON
No. No. No.

(His gaze lands on the
  bookshelf.)

I mean, I don't think so.

THOMAS
You don't "think" so? Dr. Simon, surely you can't--

SIMON
Oh, no. I am sure she's not.

(to THOMAS)
Right?

(THOMAS tilts is head in
  disbelief)

Right...Um...It's almost certainly dissociative. I don't know what else it could be.

THOMAS
Trigger?

SIMON
Hard to say. We seemed to be going along just fine until...

THOMAS
Yes...?

SIMON
(Reflecting.)
We mentioned school.

THOMAS
Performance anxiety? Social complex?

SIMON
Maybe.

(REBECCA returns)

REBECCA
She's freshening up. So...?

SIMON
I honestly haven't a clue. She could be dissociative. She could be acting. She could be...

REBECCA
Possessed?

SIMON
I doubt it.
(repeats pointedly to THOMAS)
I doubt it.

REBECCA
What then?

SIMON
At this point I am just not sure. I am sure, though, that she needs more than what we have to offer here.

REBECCA
In house, Simon. Hardesty was very clear in that regard.

SIMON
I know, but Rebecca, she might be in danger.

REBECCA
From whom?

SIMON
From herself. She said "She's going away." That's a quote. When...whatever was happening... was happening, that's what she said. "She's going away."

REBECCA
Suicide? Cry for help?

THOMAS
Or attention.

SIMON
Whichever. We shouldn't run that risk.

                    REBECCA
Simon, do you truly believe that she is in imminent danger?
Please, be honest. Do you think she was sending a message?

                     SIMON
In that condition, who can say for sure?

                    REBECCA
We want her safe, but I don't want to push any unnecessary
alarms. Once something like that is out of the bag....

                     SIMON
There's no putting it back.

                    REBECCA
And if we have to bring anyone else in on this--

                     SIMON
I know. I know. But still.

           (Katie reenters)

                    REBECCA
I can try to keep her in Jennifer's room for a few more days. That
way somebody is watching, but after last night--

           (KATIE has walked back in)

                     KATIE
I don't need a baby sitter, Professor.

                    REBECCA
No, Katie, no one is saying that.

                     KATIE
Sounds that way to me.

                     SIMON
Katie, what I think Professor Collins was suggesting was that, for
your own safety, maybe it would be best if you continued to stay
with your Resident Advisor until your sleepwalking is under
control. Surely you can understand how dangerous that could be.

                     KATIE
I guess so. I just...don't want to feel like some weird specimen.

                        REBECCA
You won't. I'll go check to make sure that Jennifer's there. I'll
come back, and then we can get you settled in. Alright?

                        KATIE
Yeah. Okay.

                        SIMON
We'll relax over a nice cup of tea. We'll be fine. Right, Katie?

                        KATIE
                    (unconvinced)
Sure.

                        REBECCA
I'll be right back.

                    (KATIE doesn't look up.
                     REBECCA shoots SIMON and
                     concerned look. He encourages
                     her to go indicating all will be
                     well.)

                        SIMON
Well, I'll just get the water going.

                    (SIMON removes his jacket and
                     steps into the back room with
                     the tea kettle.)

                        KATIE
Thanks, Dr. Reed.

                    (KATIE curls up onto her chair.
                     She seems vulnerable and
                     unsure of what is coming next.
                     THOMAS keeps a wary, clinical
                     eye on her.)

So am I your first "haunted" girl?

                        THOMAS
I don't think you're haunted.

                        KATIE
                    (genuinely relieved)
Thanks.

THOMAS

I think you're very troubled.

KATIE

Oh.

THOMAS

I just meant--

KATIE

I know what you meant.

THOMAS
(awkward pause)

Um...I guess I should...uh...would you tell Dr. Reed I'll be back in a minute?

KATIE

Sure.

(THOMAS leaves. SIMON comes strolling back in wiping his hands on a small towel.)

SIMON

Thomas, let's reschedule...

(He Looks up and realizes THOMAS has gone.)

Oh.

KATIE

He said he'd be right back.

SIMON

Alright then.

(He makes his way back to his desk and casually flips through a file on his desk, presumably hers. He closes it resolutely. Meanwhile, KATIE has again taken the perch stance on her chair.)

Let's just chat, shall we? No files. No inquisition. Just talk. That will be fun, huh?

(SIMON turns and is startled to see KATIE in place.)

                              KATIE
Chat. Chat. Chat. Chat...
                              (SIMON slowly makes his way
                              toward her a step or two.
                              KATIE begins to giggle
                              ominously which stops him in
                              his tracks. They stare at each
                              other for a beat. Without
                              warning, two shelves of books
                              on either side of the desk eject
                              their books into the room.
                              SIMON, ducks and slowly
                              returns to his feet. KATIE
                              simply smiles.)
Fun, huh?
                              (THOMAS returns and looks
                              around the room, shocked at
                              the scene. SIMON stands
                              transfixed and unsure. KATIE
                              grins. BLACKOUT)

ACT II

SCENE ONE

> Early the next day. The office looks basically the same with the exception of a love seat that has been brought in and placed between the chairs. SIMON sits at his desk pouring over text after text. He occasionally finds something of interests, highlights or underlines it, and then moves onto another book.
>
> THOMAS enters carrying coffee he has picked up and a bag of breakfast. He immediately sets one of the cups on SIMON'S desk.

SIMON

Thanks.

THOMAS

Another long night?

SIMON

Yes. Yes. We had Katie here until early this morning.

THOMAS

Anything new?

SIMON

Not from her but...

> (He holds up one of the folders.)

I did find something of interest in the family history. She mentioned her brother and sister, but she failed to mention she was a twin.

THOMAS

So she lied.

SIMON

Not necessarily.

                    THOMAS
How is that possible? She said the brother was older, and the sister was younger.

                    SIMON
And both those statements are true. Hers, if you choose to categorize it as such, is not a lie of commission but rather a lie of omission. She simply did not tell us that she was a twin.

                    THOMAS
So where is the other?

                    SIMON
Well, that is the interesting part. The other twin, she died before birth.

                    THOMAS
What is the significance of that?

                         (SIMON hands him a large book,
                          already opened to a book-
                          marked page. THOMAS reads
                          aloud.)
Twin-twin transfusion?

                    SIMON
Yes, TTT involves one child literally feeding off of nutrients needed by another child.

                    THOMAS
Like a pre-natal vampire?

                    SIMON
Well, it's nothing that sinister I assure you. It's simply a matter of necessary elements being diverted to one child while the other is deprived.

                    THOMAS
Survivor's guilt?

                    SIMON
Perhaps. If you think about it, that is a potentially heavy emotional burden with which to weigh yourself.

THOMAS
Unless that is exactly what she wants us to see.

SIMON
True enough. Did you ever get those transcripts for me?

(THOMAS jumps up and grabs some papers from his bag. He shuttles them to SIMON.)

THOMAS
I put freshman year in with the family med files...

SIMON
(interjecting)
I got those.

THOMAS
...and these I picked up this morning.

SIMON
High school?

THOMAS
Yup.

SIMON
(scans them quickly)
Let's see...

THOMAS
What are you looking for exactly?

SIMON
Oh, something like...

(He stops scanning having obviously found that for which he was looking.)

This.

(THOMAS anxiously looks expecting some great revelation.)

THOMAS
Okay, what am I looking at?

SIMON

Junior and Senior electives.

> (THOMAS closely examines. He smiles.)

THOMAS

Theater.

SIMON
(nodding)

Theater.

THOMAS

Acting I, Acting II, Introduction to Theater...she was a drama geek.

SIMON

Yes, indeed. And a limber drama geek at that. Don't forget her gymnastic and dance experience.

THOMAS

You don't buy the act do you?

SIMON

I'm keeping all options open.

> (There is a knock at the door.)

THOMAS
(makes his way to answer the door)

And to think I was beginning to doubt you. I have a new respect for you method of inquiry.

> (He opens the door and a priest, FATHER DENNIS ARMSTRONG, enters. He is roughly the same age as SIMON and, in street clothes, could easily be mistaken for the husband or father next door.)

SIMON
(crossing to greet his friend)

Dennis!

DENNIS
Simon...

THOMAS
Well, that was short-lived.

(The comment does not go
unnoticed by SIMON who
crosses to greet his friend.)

DENNIS
I came as soon as I got your message. I thought talking in person might be better.

THOMAS
Why is there a priest here, Simon? What exactly does he want to talk about?

SIMON AND DENNIS
(together)
Nothing.

THOMAS
Are you sure this isn't about--?

SIMON AND DENNIS
(offering wholesale denials)
Oh, no no no. Of course not.

THOMAS
(unconvinced)
Well it better not be. Because if Dean Hardesty were to hear about that...It's bad enough that some people actually believe this condition to be some sort of weird magic. The last thing we need is to bring in some hocus pocus to pretend to treat it.

SIMON
Dennis is an old...

(emphasizing the point for
humor)

...a VERY old...

(The joke is not lost on Dennis
who smiles.)

...friend. He is here to check up on me.

DENNIS
This is true.

THOMAS
Well, it better be. Because if Dean Hardesty--

SIMON
Thomas, why don't you see what you can find in junior high files? In the back.
(THOMAS simply shakes his head as he accepts his banishment.)

THOMAS
Hocus pocus.

DENNIS
Open minded young man?

SIMON
Oh it's decidedly open...to any and all things non-religious. Sit. Sit.

(DENNIS takes a seat as SIMON pours coffee. THOMAS stares intently.)

I appreciate your stopping by.

(He notices THOMAS' glare.)

Thought you were out of town for the week. Left you a message but--

DENNIS
Yeah, I was back home for a few days. But I'm officiating a wedding this weekend and had a few details to finalize. In fact, that's where I am headed now.

SIMON
Well, I'm glad to see you. I really needed to talk about this case.

DENNIS
It sounded like it.

SIMON
Maybe I just needed to refill my spiritual cup, and mass alone wasn't going to cut it.

DENNIS
Yeah? I haven't seen you at mass recently.

SIMON
Well, the holidays are coming so...

(SIMON hands the coffee to
DENNIS and sits beside him)

Plus, Elizabeth hasn't been feeling up to it.

DENNIS
Yes. I got an e-mail from her a few weeks ago. Gotta a name yet?

SIMON
Yes, we do.

DENNIS
Gonna tell me what it is?

SIMON
No, I'm not.

DENNIS
Come on. If you can't trust a priest, who can you trust?

SIMON
I'll tell you at the Christening.

DENNIS
Nice.

SIMON
Oh, it's just, with all the complications, there still seems to be such a long way to go. And if we share too much and anything goes wrong--

DENNIS
Oh, I understand. Any official word yet?

SIMON
No. No. Everyone is still as clueless as they were four months ago.

DENNIS
I'm sorry. I thought sure that, by now, they'd have answers.

SIMON
So did we. But, listen, I didn't call you here to talk about my problems.

DENNIS
You sure about that?

SIMON
Quite. Look, about the girl--

DENNIS
Yes, yes. I know. The "scary girl". But it is odd, you know? There are many people you could have called. The Cardinal Neuman center on campus. Other psychologists.

SIMON
(standing and heading behind
his desk)
Look, if you don't want to help--

DENNIS
I didn't say I don't want to help. I just think you need to be more clear about just whom I am helping.
(THOMAS has returned and has
a keen interest in what
DENNIS is saying)

SIMON
(somewhat nervously shuffling
papers)
Dennis, what are you talking about?

DENNIS
Look, this girl's situation -- I am guessing -- is unique. It's unusual, even for you. So, you've checked your journals?

SIMON
Yup.

DENNIS
The texts?

SIMON
Of course.

DENNIS
Run it by colleagues?

SIMON
Yes. I mean it was more for the sake of verifying--

DENNIS
Have you prayed on it?

SIMON
Excuse me?

(THOMAS is now very interested in the turn this conversation has taken.)

DENNIS
You're a Christian.

SIMON
Yes.

DENNIS
Have you prayed on it?

(THOMAS squares his chair in SIMON's direction, very curious as to what he will say. SIMON, becomes somewhat self-conscious of that fact and hesitates in stating his answer.)

SIMON
Well...

DENNIS
Sometimes silence speaks volumes. Simon, this...situation -- if it is anywhere close to what you described -- is going to require someone of tremendous strength. Someone whose faith is solid. Someone willing to trust in the Lord, implicitly.

SIMON
Are you offering to step in?

DENNIS
Well, as you don't have the authority of your superiors to even disclose what we aren't talking about...

SIMON
True enough.

DENNIS
And since my superiors -- to say nothing of THEIR superiors way, way back across the pond -- won't even officially recognize this topic, publicly at least, I am guessing that won't be happening.

SIMON
So? Truthfully, what do you think?

DENNIS
Truthfully? I think the world is full of things that we can't explain. Good and bad alike. The good we ascribe to God. To Christ. And to angels and the intervention of saints or the Blessed Mother. But the bad...well, the bad is something else.

SIMON
Evil?

DENNIS
Evil. And when that evil happens many times people forget that it too comes from somewhere. And since nothing evil can come from God, it has to come from someone...something...else. And that something else is beyond anything in your books or journals. And it requires help that only God can provide.

SIMON
Dennis, I don't know how much pull I have upstairs.

DENNIS
It's not about pull, it's about faith. And one of the biggest acts of faith we can make, and thus one of the greatest acts of worship we can perform, is to turn our troubles and doubts and questions over to God so that He can guide us, comfort us, and answer us in our trials and tribulations. So I'm asking -- believer to believer, Christian to Christian, brother to brother-- have you prayed on it?

THOMAS
He's a psychologist not a monk.

DENNIS
Oh, I know. Full head of hair is a dead giveaway.

THOMAS
Father, I don't think this is a laughing matter.

SIMON
Thomas...

    (SIMON is clearly uncomfortable
    with THOMAS overstepping his
    bounds and moves to hush
    him. DENNIS waves him off to
    allow THOMAS to continue.)

THOMAS
Respectfully, Dr. Reed, I don't think it fair for you to try and protect him here.

SIMON
Oh, it wasn't him I was trying to protect.

    (SIMON now casually pulls up a
    chair and begins to watch the
    debate, sipping his coffee.)

Do continue.

THOMAS
    (somewhat confused by the
    statement)
A young lady is clearly suffering...something...and asking Dr. Reed if he has "prayed on it" undermines not only the seriousness of the situation but the seriousness of our profession.

DENNIS
It was certainly not my intention to discount your efforts or the work you do.

THOMAS
Thank you.

DENNIS
Although it would appear that is precisely your intention toward mine.

THOMAS
We are dealing in facts.

DENNIS
And by inference, I am meant to understand that we -- people of faith -- deal in fiction?

                    THOMAS
Father, I mean no disrespect...

                    DENNIS
                (to SIMON)
Why is it when people say "I mean no disrespect..." you can be certain they are about to illustrate a tremendous amount of disrespect?
                (SIMON smiles and continues to
                 enjoy both his coffee and the
                 impending conversation.)
You were saying...?

                    THOMAS
                (unsure how to react and
                 shifting his gaze between
                 DENNIS who listens patiently
                 and SIMON who seems
                 bemused)
...um...I...was just...saying....I was just...
                (steeling himself)
I was just saying that I basically respect the work that you do. And I respect the fact that you have faith in a system which encourages that work. But in the end it remains...faith.

                    DENNIS
As opposed to science?

                    THOMAS
Yes.

                    DENNIS
Which is more factual?

                    THOMAS
Correct.

                    DENNIS
Orderly?

                    THOMAS
Uh-huh.

DENNIS
And completely unable to exist outside the conceptual framework of spirituality?

THOMAS
Right...wait. Huh?

DENNIS
Well, think about it. For science to be recognized as "true", some kind of absolute value system has to be in place.

THOMAS
Well, sure but--

DENNIS
And for that absolute value system to have any credence, certain philosophical assumptions must be made.

THOMAS
Uh...

DENNIS
Don't hurt yourself. And for those philosophical assumptions to be made truthfully, the Christian world view needs to be employed.

THOMAS
Why?

DENNIS
Well, the laws of logic, the orderly nature of the external world, the reliability of our cognitive faculties to say nothing of the moral values are all constructs which, strictly speaking, are unable to be proven scientifically...

THOMAS
(looking for a chance to
interject)
But--

DENNIS
(without ceding)
...yet depend upon the guarantee of a Christian world view in which to thrive. A writer, a science writer -- Loren Eisley, said that science is an "invented cultural institution" requiring "unique soil" in which to grow. His point? That this environment, a decidedly Christian environment, gave birth to the experimental scientific

DENNIS (CONT'D)
method. Basically, for us to place our trust in anything, we have to establish "truth". To establish truth, we need to have some universal baseline. And, for that universal baseline to exist at all, well thank God -- figuratively and literally.

(THOMAS stands motionless. He looks to SIMON for some guidance. SIMON merely gestures that he should sit which the assistant does, very slowly.)

SIMON
Was that really necessary?

DENNIS
(returning to his seat)
Probably not, but it was fun.

SIMON
No.

DENNIS
No?

SIMON
No, I haven't prayed on it.

DENNIS
Maybe you should.

SIMON
I haven't done that in a long time.

DENNIS
That's the thing about God, Simon. He's always there no matter where you are. Look, I know how this sounds to a guy in your position, but while it may very well be any of those fancy names you rattled off on the phone, what if it isn't? What if it is exactly what it seems to be?

SIMON
It can't be...

DENNIS
If it is, then you have to have your house in order, spiritually speaking. This will be a test of not only your abilities but your faith. And when I say "faith", I don't mean the little niceties that fill your mind on those two special days a year you decide to break the parish threshold. I am talking about the core beliefs that somewhere, way down deep, you either hold true or not. Your core beliefs about good and evil.

SIMON
Dennis, this is...I don't know what this is, and that's a new place for me to be. Now I've already identified some factors that point to this being a simple case induced by pre-natal Twin-Twin Transference. It's probably nothing more than guilt manifesting itself in these mini-dramas--

DENNIS
Mini-dramas you call parents. Possessions you call a priest. I'm a priest.
(SIMON self-consciously looks at
THOMAS who stares with
condemnation.)

SIMON
Yeah, I know. But she's a gymnast and an actress and a high strung surviving twin who basically might have fed off a sibling to make it into this world. That's a lot to work with in and of itself. What if she has some kind of deep self-loathing, and she's dissociative? What if it's some attention-getting ploy because daddy didn't love her enough? And what if--?

DENNIS
...she is an unwitting host to forces beyond natural explanation?

SIMON
Dennis, there are so many variables.

DENNIS
Lex parsimoniae.

SIMON
Occam's razor.

THOMAS
(hesitantly)
What's Occam's razor?

SIMON
The law of parsimony...the law of economy...the law of succinctness...when you have two competing theories that make exactly the same predictions--

DENNIS
...the simpler one is the better. Can you come up with anything simpler than good old fashioned possession?

SIMON
There are so many questions--

DENNIS
That she seems to be answering perched on desks, walls, and ceilings.

SIMON
There are books--

DENNIS
Flying off of your shelves and across dorm rooms.

SIMON
So, you're saying--?

DENNIS
Nope. I'm not saying anything...officially. That's a bit above my pay grade. But if I were to say anything--

SIMON
Don't.
(He sighs audibly.)

It just doesn't seem possible. Not in the 21st Century, you know?

DENNIS
"It will come about after this. That I will pour My Spirit on all mankind; And your sons and daughters will prophesy, Your old men will dream dreams, Your young men will see visions..."

SIMON
Dennis. She's a limber young girl with a flair for the dramatic. And it's up to me to help her before she hurts herself. And I am not a priest.

DENNIS
"And God did extraordinary miracles through Paul, so that even handkerchiefs and aprons that had touched him were taken to the sick, and their illnesses were cured and the evil spirits left them..."

SIMON
I am no Paul.

DENNIS
"Some Jews who went around driving out evil spirits tried to invoke the name of the Lord Jesus over those who were demon-possessed. They would say, 'In the name of the Jesus whom Paul preaches, I command you to come out'--"

SIMON
"And ...One day the evil spirit answered them, "Jesus I know, and Paul I know about, but who are you?' Then the man who had the evil spirit jumped on them and overpowered them all. He gave them such a beating that they ran out of the house naked and bleeding--"

DENNIS
Somebody's been studying up.

SIMON
All options.

(pointedly to THOMAS)

All. Options.

(THOMAS retreats to the relative safety of his desk.)

Dennis, there is a chance that this is no more than a confused kid crying out for attention or help or whatever, and I am doing my due diligence to that end.

DENNIS
But...?

SIMON
But...if I am going to be intellectually honest about this...

(glances at THOMAS)

And keep all options truly open, then I know that there are other schools of thought I should entertain.

DENNIS
Is it something you're up for?

SIMON
Do I have a choice?

DENNIS
(stands and shakes SIMON's
hand and hands him a Bible)

We all have a choice.

(He begins to walk out. THOMAS
has watched him carefully.
DENNIS stops and looks over
his shoulder at THOMAS.)

We all have a choice.

THOMAS
(rises and exits toward the back
room, phone in hand)

Dean Hardesty will hear about this. All of this.

SIMON
I have no doubt.

DENNIS
You had better not have.

(DENNIS leaves. SIMON opens
the Bible. THOMAS glares
disapprovingly. FADE TO
BLACK.)

SCENE TWO

> Lights Up. It is evening of that same day. KATIE is positioned on the couch. SIMON is in his usual chair, and REBECCA is standing opposite him, watching over KATIE who is clearly in one of her "states". THOMAS is standing next to her.

KATIE

So brave. You have to have the little woman with you.

> (laughs)

As if that will help.

> (KATIE pretends to lunge at REBECCA does not flinch but ultimately steps back quite far.)

Boo!

> (Katie again laughs diabolically.)

SIMON

Sit down.

KATIE
(mimicking)

Sit down. Oh so stern. He runs such a tight ship. Are you the captain of this ship? The doctor is the captain of this ship. The captain. The captain. Aye aye, Captain.

> (REBECCA cautiously resumes her position and looks at THOMAS who has not moved.)

THOMAS
(smugly)

Professionals don't flinch.

REBECCA

Simon. I am so sorry. I was just startled.

SIMON

You have nothing to apologize for. She--

KATIE
(seemingly insulted)
I should be offended--

SIMON
He--

KATIE
(indicating herself)
She should be offended.

SIMON
It--

KATIE
Closer--

SIMON
It wants you to be fearful...and apologetic. Be neither.

KATIE
Yes, be neither. But be nearer...

REBECCA
(again unnerved)
Simon...?

SIMON
Go. Go. Take a break. Thomas, escort Professor Collins would you. And then come right back.

REBECCA
(leaving)
I am so sorry...

KATIE
There she goes again.

REBECCA
(pausing at the door)
What is this?

KATIE
THIS IS WHAT YOU THINK IT IS! AND I AM WHO WISH I WASN'T!

(REBECCA freezes, and SIMON indicates that she should go. REBECCA closes the door quickly. KATIE spins in her seat.)

KATIE (CONT'D)
And then there were two.

SIMON
That's it? Two? Traveling light these days.

KATIE
Don't play with me, or I will keep her when she goes.

SIMON
You've taken to picking on little girls now, have you?

KATIE
You have no idea.

SIMON
Oh, I've some.

KATIE
Well then, doctor, come sit by me, and share your ideas. Unless you are afraid.

SIMON
Why should I be afraid?

KATIE
Tick tock. Tick tock. Time is fleeting.

SIMON
For everyone. And everything. Now, I don't want to ruin it for you, but I've read the book. Things end poorly for you.

KATIE
And those I take with me. So glib but so naive. You have no idea what awaits.

SIMON
Am I to infer a threat?

KATIE
Make of it what you will. She is slipping away.

SIMON
Why do you want a college student?

KATIE
I don't!

SIMON
Then let her be.

KATIE
I can't!

SIMON
You'll be disappointed.

KATIE
(smiling)
I won't...

SIMON
It could have been anyone. Why her?

KATIE
Why don't you answer that? Doc-TOR! Tick tock.

(SIMON crosses to the door and cautiously peers down the hallway. Assured that no one is approaching, SIMON turns and begins to speak in Latin with both urgency and authority.)

SIMON
Exorcizo te, omnis spiritus immunde, in nomine Dei Patris omnipotentis...

(Katie snaps her head toward him in surprise and begins to squirm uncomfortably.)

...et in nominae Jesu Christi Filii ejus, Domini et Judicis nostri,...

(KATIE is now writhing on the love seat)

KATIE

No. Stop it! Stop!

SIMON

...et in virtute Spiritus Sancti, ut descedas ab hoc plasmate Dei Katie,...

    (KATIE screams as if in agony. Her body seems to physical distend and distort with each passing word.)

...quod Dominus noster ad templum sanctum suumvocare dignatus est...

KATIE

I am warning you--

    (She buries her head in her hands, screaming and rolling as if in pain.)

SIMON

    (SIMON has moved progressively closer and is now standing over KATIE behind the love seat.)

...ut fiat templum Dei vivi,...

KATIE

Nooooooooooooooo!

    (THOMAS and REBECCA enter. She rushes to the couch beside SIMON. THOMAS freezes at the sight of the ritual taking place.)

THOMAS

What are you doing?

SIMON

...et Spiritus Sanctum habitat in eo...

    (KATIE's thrashing intensifies as she seems to almost alternate between screaming and crying.)

                        REBECCA
                    (to THOMAS)
Get over here! Now!
                    (THOMAS rushes to help
                        REBECCA. They both want to
                        hold KATIE down but are afraid
                        to hurt her so they seem,
                        instead, to shadow her
                        motions.)

                        SIMON
...Per enumdem Christum Dominum nostrum...
                    (The phone begins to ring.
                        REBECCA runs to it.)

                        REBECCA
I'll get it. Might be security.
                    (KATIE is sobbing loudly now
                        with virtually no break until it
                        begins to turn rhythmic.)

                        SIMON
Qui venturas est judicare vivos et mortuos, et saeculum per ignem!

                    (REBECCA is on the phone while
                        THOMAS, in disbelief, seeks to
                        make sense of the events.
                        KATIE's sobbing is now
                        completely rhythmic and
                        seems somehow different. It is
                        staccato. It is a laugh. She
                        lowers her hands and sits up.
                        Her laugh is boisterous and
                        derisive.)

                        KATIE
Surely you didn't believe simply parroting words would end this fun now did you.
                    (SIMON is staring, stunned.)

Ephpeta, quod est, Adaperire!

                    (She touches her nose mocking
                        the ritual.)

                    KATIE (CONT'D)
In odorem suavitatis. Tu autem effugare, diabole; appropinquabit
enim judicium Dei.
                    (KATIE laughs again)

I've heard it before. Now, it's her turn. We'll see to it
that she can recite them along with us. Oooh, she's
going away. She's going so quickly.

                    SIMON
You won't get this girl.

                    KATIE
This girl? This. Girl. I don't want THIS girl!

                    REBECCA
               (holding the phone out to him)
Simon?

                    KATIE
You know who. Look inside. You know. Don't you?

                    REBECCA
Simon.

                    SIMON
Rebecca, please. Take a mess--

                    REBECCA
It's Liz. She needs to talk to you.
                    (SIMON grabs the phone and
                    listens intently. His body
                    seems to deflate.)

                    KATIE
She's going away. She's going away. She's going away...
                    (SIMON collapses into his chair.)
And. She's. Gone.

                    THOMAS
Who are you talking about?
                    (REBECCA turns to listen)

                        KATIE
                  (indicating SIMON)
His daughter. Little Sarah...

                              (KATIE smiles. THOMAS and
                              REBECCA stare at SIMON who
                              has collapsed completely in his
                              chair. BLACKOUT.)

SCENE THREE

> It is early the next morning. THOMAS is intermittently dozing in his chair. REBECCA is leaning against SIMON's desk. They have obviously been there all night as they have not changed. DEAN HARDESTY walks in.

HARDESTY
Good morning, Rebecca.

REBECCA
Dean.

HARDESTY
You look exhausted.

REBECCA
Long night.

HARDESTY
That's what I hear. Is Simon--?

REBECCA
No. He went to be with Liz. He should be on his way back any time, though.

HARDESTY
Uh, good. Good. I had hoped to have a word with him. I was concerned.

REBECCA
Yeah.

> (THOMAS stirs and realized the Dean is in the room. He stumbles to his feet.)

THOMAS
Dean Hardesty.

> (wiping the sleep from his eyes)

Good morning.

HARDESTY
Thank you for your call. I appreciate your keeping me in the loop.

(He looks to REBECCA.)

It seems I had not been fully apprised.

REBECCA
Ah. So when you say you were concerned, you didn't so much mean you were concerned with the fact that a member of staff just lost a child as you did that someone might hear that we might have a possessed student?

HARDESTY
Well, of course I am concerned about Simon and...um--

REBECCA
Liz. Her name is Elizabeth. And the child they lost was a little girl. Sarah.

HARDESTY
Yes, well, while that news is certainly tragic, the business of education marches on. And when a bit of that business threatens to take a toll on the financial portion of that same business...well let's just say that I have a very vested interest in what is happening. Now what I would like is for someone to tell me that we are in the process of putting this whole episode behind us.

THOMAS
Yes, sir. I am seeing to it personally.

REBECCA
Oh you're seeing to it personally are you?

THOMAS
I am.
(to HARDESTY)

Someone had to. Everyone, including Dr. Reed, seemed to be getting caught up in some pseudo-metaphysical God versus devil nonsense.

REBECCA
Hmm. You know, I always got a bit of a weasely vibe from you, but I never pictured you as throwing someone under the bus. And, Tom, I think the 92% of this country that professes some kind of

REBECCA (CONT'D)
faith might take issue with your dismissing their beliefs as "pseudo-metaphysical".

THOMAS
Respectfully, Professor, this is the 21st Century.

REBECCA
Respectfully, Tom, you are an--

HARDESTY
Rebecca that's enough. Thomas has a point. This university cannot be viewed as buying into the idea that this story is somehow supernatural in origin. Moreover, it certainly cannot be seen as actually endorsing some medieval rite as the panacea. Our position as a university could not be more clear. And I have to know where he stands right now. The Board of Chancellors wants answers. They want to know where his loyalties lie. They need to know that we are all on the same page.

REBECCA
Well, Dean...oh, and Tom, my very dear friend is facing some of the darkest moments of his life right now. As is his beautiful, patient, and formerly hopeful wife. What they need to do is take some time, together, to face this situation and heal. Yet, instead, he is coming back here to help a young lady who seems to be at the mercy of something we either don't or won't understand. This despite the fact that he neither wanted nor asked for this burden. So I'd say his loyalty is not in question. And my position as a friend could not be more clear. So, I am going to continue to sit here and keep them both in my thoughts and prayers. And if for some reason either of you has a problem with that, well, I suggest you take it up with a much higher authority than the Board of Chancellors.

THOMAS
Dean Hardesty, I have the young lady under constant supervision and a network of analysts on call waiting to hear that the all-clear has been given and --

HARDESTY
Thomas, later.

>   (At that, SIMON walks in. He is a
>   little taken aback to see everyone
>   waiting on him.)

REBECCA
How is Liz?

SIMON
She's...alright. Hanging in as best as can be expected.

HARDESTY
That's good to hear, Simon.

>   (SIMON shoots a glare at
>   THOMAS)

SIMON
Thank you, Dean Hardesty.

THOMAS
I called the dean. I thought--

>   (REBECCA simply shakes her
>   head, stopping his sentence in
>   mid-thought.)

REBECCA
You've done enough thinking for one day.

THOMAS
Dean Hardesty, I am a professional and I don't have to stand here and--

HARDESTY
Actually, can you both give us a moment?

THOMAS
Fine. I was just going to get the subject--

REBECCA
>   (She starts toward the door.)

Katie. Her name is Katie. And I will go get her. I don't want you turning her into a case study between here and the quad.

                             HARDESTY
Rebecca, why don't you let Thomas get her? We should have a
conversation as well.

                             REBECCA
You know what Dean? We really shouldn't. Not unless you want to
explain to the Board why you now need to find replacement
tenured professor and dorm supervisor.

                             HARDESTY
Are you threatening to quit?

                             REBECCA
Nope. Promising. I'd give me a wide berth, Franklin.

             (She walks to SIMON, hugs him,
              and gives him a light kiss on
              the cheek.)

Call me if you need anything.

             (As she turns to walk out, she
              glares at the dean who takes a
              very pronounced step back.
              REBECCA laughs to herself.)

Good to see we're on the same page after all.

             (As she walks by THOMAS who
              is holding the door, REBECCA
              does a quick feint in his
              direction causing him to jump.
              She laughs as she leaves.)

Professionals don't flinch.

             (REBECCA exits.)

                             HARDESTY
Simon, I thought--

             (HARDESTY and SIMON are both
              suddenly aware of THOMAS
              who is still standing in the
              room, a very obvious fly on the
              wall.)

That will be all for now, Thomas.

HARDESTY (CONT'D)
(A disappointed Thomas makes his way out of the room. He steadfastly avoids making eye contact with SIMON.)

I thought we had an understanding.

SIMON

We had an agreement. You asked me to see if I could help this young lady quietly and on my own.

HARDESTY

And?

SIMON

I couldn't.

HARDESTY

So you called in a priest?

SIMON

I consulted an old friend.

HARDESTY

Who happens to be a priest.

SIMON

Yes.

HARDESTY

How is that keeping this off of the radar?

SIMON

As a friend, he will keep it to himself. As a priest, he will keep it to himself. And as someone who answers to the Vatican, well, let's just say, he has no incentive to stir that hornet's nest.

HARDESTY

Can you hear yourself, Simon? You are a psychologist. A scientist. A man of reason.

SIMON

All of those things are true. And as a psychologist, I spoke with her. As a scientist, I did my research. And as someone reasonable,

SIMON (CONT'D)
I am using what evidence is presented to draw my conclusions -- not basing them on Deans, Boards, Chancellors, or public opinion.

HARDESTY
Simon, listen to me--

SIMON
No, Franklin, you listen to me. You asked me to do a job, and I am doing it to the best of my ability. It's called "science" not "scientism". I don't put my faith in the method. I put it in the information yielded. And one cannot simply rewrite the question if they don't like the answers.

HARDESTY
Then let me give you the only answer I want. The girl is now fine, and if she isn't fine, we will put her into contact with the proper medical officials to make certain that she is.

SIMON
And if I don't believe that?

HARDESTY
Simon, medical bills are expensive. This is not the time to lose benefits...or salary.
   (The threat hits home.)

Think of your wife. She needs you right now. She can't afford...you can't afford...any additional hardships.

   (SIMON says nothing.)

Put away this exorcism nonsense. Quit calling priests and any subsequent attention to this situation. Save prayers for Sunday, and just go back to the business of being a doctor.

   (Beat)

You are a respected member of this community, Simon. Please let it stay that way. For all our sakes.

   (HARDESTY heads for the door.)

When Thomas brings the girl back, refer her to someone...anyone. Make whatever excuse you deem necessary. But if I find out you

HARDESTY (CONT'D)
make any further attempt to..."cure" her, pack your things, because you will be finished here.

> (HARDESTY starts to leave and then stops short.)

And, Simon, if I find out that you are employing any more, shall we say "unconventional" methods, you will be finished *EVERY*where.

> (HARDESTY exits. SIMON takes in what was said and slowly drifts toward the window. He stares silently. He looks around the room and considers for a moment before dropping to his knees. He begins to pray.)

SIMON
Lord, I know I have not done this as often as I probably should have. I know that I have not been a light on the footpath for others where You are concerned, but I ask You to please look into my heart and know that I am here for You. And I ask, now, that You please be here with me for the sake of this young lady. Be she simply in need of guidance or in desperate need for deliverance, please let me do as You desire. Lord, please show me what I should do.

> (He starts to rise, and then slowly lowers himself to one knee.)

And, Lord, please give me the strength that Liz needs right now as we hold fast to the comfort that Sarah may be experience the joy and wonder of your eternal goodness in the hopes that one day we will all be reunited by Your grace. I trust in you, Lord. Now, please, show me the way. Amen.

> (At that, the door opens and THOMAS leads KATIE toward the love seat. SIMON stands and approaches her.)

THOMAS
Why don't you have a seat?

KATIE
(She runs to SIMON.)
Dr. Reed, Thomas says that you won't be working with me anymore. Is that true?
(SIMON is visibly angry at the
 presumption of THOMAS who
 looks away so as not to make
 eye contact.)

SIMON
Katie--

KATIE
Did I do something?

SIMON
No, of course not. How did she do today?

THOMAS
(still avoiding looking at SIMON)
So far, so good.

KATIE
One quiet morning? And you're all done helping me?

SIMON
Katie, no...it is a good start, right? And, who knows? Maybe you can string a few of these together and get yourself back on track--

KATIE
But--

SIMON
Look, the university...that is to say I...think we have gone about as far as we can together...here...in this setting.

KATIE
(somewhat distantly)
In this setting...
(SIMON realizes what is
 beginning to happen. He is also
 aware that it is going
 unnoticed by THOMAS who

> seems to be pouting across the
> room)

KATIE (CONT'D)

Please, Dr. Reed. I don't want to have to explain this to someone new. You even said we were making progress.

SIMON

We are...were.

KATIE

We were. We were. Were we?

> (KATIE appears to be slipping
> back into her state but
> momentarily gains clarity and
> pleads with SIMON.)

Dr. Reed..!

> THOMAS, startled by the urgency in
> her force, rushed beside KATIE and
> tries to physically assist her in taking
> a seat.

THOMAS

Katie--

> (With a sweeping gesture of her
> arm, KATIE brushed him away
> as if his body had no more heft
> than a gum wrapper floating in
> the breeze. He tumbles across
> the floor and stares stunned.
> KATIE bounds onto the couch
> and stands atop one of its
> arms defiantly.)

KATIE

Oh, giving up so soon?

> (as if an internal chorus is
> commenting on the exchange)

So soon. So soon. He's giving up too soon.

> (SIMON refuses to engage and
> begins to head to THOMAS as

                    KATIE jumps down and flips
                    the love seat into his path.)

                            KATIE (CONT'D)
Answer me! Are you quitting? Oh, we will so miss you.

                         (again the chorus)

We really will. Miss you much. So much.

                            (SIMON is obviously torn about
                            what role he should assume.
                            KATIE smiles mischievously.)

Alright then, maybe baby Sarah can entertain us since her daddy
won't!

                            That is the straw. SIMON grabs his
                            Bible and wields it as a shield of
                            sorts holding it an arm's length
                            away. He begins to angrily speak in
                            Aramaic, a language unfamiliar to
                            THOMAS but obviously not to KATIE
                            in this state.

                                SIMON
Ma smuk?

                            (KATIE seems somewhat taken
                            aback.)

                                KATIE
Such an old language. Such a dead language. Such dead faith.

                                THOMAS
Simon, what are you doing?

                                SIMON
I asked her name.

                                THOMAS
In what language?

                                SIMON
Aramaic. Ma smuk?

(KATIE seems amused and
smiles. She starts to chuckle
before barking an answer.)

KATIE

Ismi aswad!

THOMAS

What did she say?

SIMON

"My name is black." How many of you are there?

KATIE
(bounding atop a chair)
Wahid. Ithnaan. Thalatha. Khamsoon. Sitton. Mi'a!

THOMAS

How many?

SIMON

"One. Two. Three. Fifty. Sixty. One hundred."

(THOMAS has slowly inched up
against the office door. SIMON,
emboldened by the exchange,
strides ever closer.)

You are finished here. You have no place here in this child of God. He who sent His son Jesus Christ to die for our sins.

KATIE

Oh, such sin!

SIMON

You will depart this child. I command you in the name of Jesus Christ.

KATIE

Abadan!

SIMON
(He looks to THOMAS who is
confused. SIMON fills him in on
what she is saying.)
"Never".

                        KATIE

He took your little girl.

                (chiding with bitter glee)

The little one. Such a little one.

                    (KATIE stands atop SIMON's
                     desk and announces with
                     consternation.)

He took her from you yet you defend Him?

                        SIMON
                      (sternly)

Da'eman!

                    (SIMON smiles)

Always!

                    (SIMON opens the Bible and
                     begins to recite from
                     Ephesians. As he does, he
                     approaches KATIE who retreats
                     slowly but surely. With each
                     word she seems to recoil in
                     pain.)

"Finally, be strong in the Lord and in his mighty power. Put on the full armor of God so that you can take your stand against the devil's schemes. For our struggle is not against flesh and blood, but against the rulers, against the authorities, against the powers of this dark world and against the spiritual forces of evil in the heavenly realms.

                        KATIE

Stop.

                        SIMON

...Therefore put on the full armor of God, so that when the day of evil comes, you may be able to stand your ground, and after you have done everything, to stand....

                    (THOMAS has scampered across
                     the floor to the safety of
                     SIMON's desk and he begins
                     frantically dialing his phone.

(KATIE has now cleared almost the length of the room.)

SIMON (CONT'D)
...Stand firm then.

KATIE
No!

SIMON
With the belt of truth buckled around your waist, with the breastplate of righteousness in place, and with your feet fitted with the readiness that comes from the gospel of peace...take up the shield of faith, with which you can extinguish all the flaming arrows of the evil one.

(KATIE is slowly sliding down the wall as if the words themselves are weighing her down.)

KATIE
Atsor! Atsor!

SIMON
...Take the helmet of salvation and the sword of the Spirit, which is the word of God. And pray in the Spirit on all occasions with all kinds of prayers and requests...

KATIE
Ghadan.

SIMON
...With this in mind, be alert and always keep on praying for all the saints. Pray also for me,...

KATIE
Ghadan!

SIMON
...that whenever I open my mouth, words may be given so that I will fearlessly...

KATIE
Ghadan.

SIMON

...As I should!"

KATIE
(collapsing into a ball on the ground screaming and laughing)

GHADAN!!!

(AT this moment **EVERY LIGHT IN THE THEATER-- house, stage, back, lobby-- goes to BLACK. Literally, every light in the building goes out for a BEAT.** Then they come back. THOMAS is shaken and looking around. SIMON cautiously approaches KATIE who seems to have come around. SIMON helps her to her feet.)

Dr. Reed...?

SIMON

It's alright, Katie.

(He brushes the hair from her eyes as he makes a quick assessment of the situation.)

It's over now.

(She looks confused. REBECCA bursts through the door.)

REBECCA

Simon?

(SIMON simply nods toward KATIE who is shaken.)

Come here, darlin'. Let's get you cleaned up.

KATIE
(KATIE is being helped out by REBECCA. KATIE stops and turns.)

Dr. Reed? Is it really over?

(He nods silently. KATIE runs to him and hugs him. REBECCA escorts her out. They exit. FADE TO BLACK.)

SCENE FOUR

> It is several days later. The room is essentially returned to the state it was at the beginning of the play. The love seat is covered. Many books on SIMON's shelf are also gone. His desk is virtually empty save for a computer monitor, light, and phone. THOMAS is at his desk and moving files from a cabinet to SIMON's desk.
>
> THOMAS briefly takes a seat in SIMON's chair but jumps up quickly as SIMON enters from the back carrying a box full of his personal belongings. He sets it on the chair nearest the door.

SIMON
Well, that should about do it.

(THOMAS seems too embarrassed to say anything.)

Go ahead. It's pretty comfortable. I understand you'll be staying on as assistant again next semester to help the new counselor transition in.

THOMAS
Yes. They decided it would be in the best interest of everyone to have someone familiar with the case load on hand--

SIMON
Oh, absolutely makes sense.

THOMAS
Did Professor Collins resign then?

SIMON
Oh no, no, no. They couldn't afford to let her go.

THOMAS
Because she's so valuable to the university?

SIMON
Because she knows where all the bones are buried.

(SIMON is taking a cursory look
around to make certain he
hasn't missed anything.)

THOMAS
You could have just let it go, you know?

SIMON
No, Thomas, I'm afraid I couldn't.

THOMAS
I thought you had landed on a diagnosis. I thought her background explained away the phenomena. And more importantly, I thought your future was worth more to you than proving a point.

SIMON
It wasn't about proving a point, Thomas.

THOMAS
Then what was it about?

SIMON
Do not be overcome by evil, but overcome evil by good.

THOMAS
Confucious?

SIMON
Paul...in a letter to the Romans.

(THOMAS sighs audibly)

Yes, I know that quoting Scripture is vile to you--

THOMAS
Not vile. Just a waste of time.

SIMON
Fair enough...and you know I hate to admit this, but before Katie I might have even agreed...whether I wanted to or not. I mean I claimed to be a person of faith, but how much did I exhibit that for others to see? You even pointed that out.

THOMAS
Why is that your job?

SIMON
Because, we...Christians...are asked to not repay evil for evil, but to take thought for what is noble in the sight of all.

THOMAS
Even if it means throwing everything away?

SIMON
I guess I don't see it that way...at least, not any more.
(THOMAS just stares blankly)
God will provide.
(THOMAS again stares without acknowledging.)
Right.
(SIMON picks up his box of belongings.)

THOMAS
Why Aramaic?

SIMON
Because she would not have known it.

THOMAS
But she did.

SIMON
Did she?
(THOMAS is somewhat put off by the inference and turns to his desk to resume sorting files and replacing them on what used to be SIMON's desk. SIMON starts to leave.)

THOMAS
You know they have asked me to write the official version. My report is going to say it was simply guilt over the Twin-Twin Transfusion manifesting itself and exacerbated by a generally unstable nature.

SIMON
You could say that...

THOMAS

Then why didn't you?

SIMON
Because she never knew.

THOMAS
What?

SIMON
The files. Her medical history. When her parents spoke with the initial analyst, they admitted that they never told her about her twin. In fact, they apparently never told anyone, including the other siblings. As far as she knows, it was only ever her.

THOMAS
You can't know that for sure.

SIMON
You comfortable putting your faith in that?

THOMAS
(starting to answer and then realizing what SIMON has set up, he shakes his head)
Yes. Very.

(SIMON begins to exit)

Simon...

SIMON
Yes?

THOMAS
What was she saying at the end? "Ghadan"?

SIMON
(smiling)
"Tomorrow".

(THOMAS seems surprised at the revelation and looks out the window.)

Goodbye, Thomas. Good luck.

(SIMON exits. THOMAS turns from the window and looks around the office which, for all intents and purposes, for now, is his alone. He smiles and walks behind SIMON's desk. THOMAS sits in the chair and tries it out for size, reclining and putting his feet up. On the shelf, a single book falls onto its spine. THOMAS, spooked looks up at it. BLACKOUT. CURTAIN.)

www.ingramcontent.com/pod-product-compliance
Lightning Source LLC
Chambersburg PA
CBHW081016040426
42444CB00014B/3232